BRITAIN IN OLD  H S

THE ISLE OF
MAN

BILL SNELLING

MANX NATIONAL HERITAGE

SUTTON PUBLISHING LIMITED

Sutton Publishing Limited
Phoenix Mill · Thrupp · Stroud
Gloucestershire · GL5 2BU

First published 1996

British Library Cataloguing in Publication Data
A catalogue record for this book is available from the
British Library.

ISBN 0-7509-1011-9

Typeset in 10/12 Perpetua.
Typesetting and origination by
Sutton Publishing Limited.
Printed in Great Britain by
Ebenezer Baylis, Worcester.

CONTENTS

The 200 ft high Warwick Revolving Tower was a short-lived attraction on Douglas Head. It cost 6*d* to be transported to the top, and offered a panoramic view across Douglas. Built in 1899, it was destroyed by fire a year later.

INTRODUCTION

The Isle of Man, situated in the Irish Sea midway between England and Ireland, has a culture and pace of life all of its own. The many surviving Celtic and Viking monuments around the island bear silent witness to the importance of the overseas marauders who came here, some to pillage and conquer, some to settle and cultivate the land, but all of them combining to leave a legacy that still persists today, and is most characteristically seen in Tynwald, our enduring thousand-year-old parliament.

Following the death of the last Viking king in 1265, sovereignty of the island passed to the Scots, but it was an unsettled period, and soon the island's strategic position in the Irish Sea became an issue in the Anglo-Scottish wars. The Isle of Man was finally annexed by England in 1346 and its government was the responsibility of a succession of English nobles before it was gifted to the Stanley family by Henry VII, grateful for their actions at the decisive Battle of Bosworth which established him on the English throne. The Stanleys and their successors, the Dukes of Atholl, ruled from 1405 to 1764, when the British Government bought the rights of ownership back in an attempt to destroy the smuggling trade for which the island had become a centre.

For centuries, farming and fishing were the main occupations of the island's population, with many families sending their menfolk away to fish during the summer months, whilst women, children and the elderly tended their stock on the hilly common lands. Mining provided alternative employment and many trial mines were dug all over Man. The main finds of lead, zinc and smaller amounts of silver came from the Laxey and Foxdale areas, but copper and iron were also found. In the 1870s and 1880s, Foxdale's lead output exceeded that of all the UK mines.

During the Victorian era, the island was 'discovered' as a holiday resort. Each year, hundreds of thousands of travellers crossed the Irish Sea on the Isle of Man Steam Packet Company's vessels, many of them coming from the industrial north, seeking respite from their daily grind in the mills and other industries. Others came from the wealthier classes, to find a haven from the pace of life in the 'adjacent isle', as the Manx folk like to call mainland Britain.

Victorian engineers built a steam railway system, which is still operational today, and together with the coastal and Snaefell summit tramways, still carries both locals and visitors, nearly a hundred years after its inception.

Motor racing came to the island in 1904, because the British Parliament would not allow roads on the mainland to be closed for racing. In 1907 the first Tourist Trophy race for motorcycles was held. This tradition continues to this day; many thousands of visitors from all over the world come to watch and compete in the greatest road races in the world.

The Manx people do not stand on ceremony; a blacksmith could become the Mayor of Douglas and a farmer the President of Tynwald.

This volume provides a brief glimpse of the history and heritage that is the Isle of Man

Niarbyl Bay. Niarbyl is Manx for 'the tail' (of rocks). In the days of farmer/fishermen, the menfolk would live down by the shore while the women and children went up into the hills with the cattle.

THE TOWN OF DOUGLAS AND ITS SUBURBS

Douglas Bay from Douglas Head, at a time when Douglas was barely developed. The Tower of Refuge can be seen standing on Conister Rock, with the fishing fleet in the outer harbour and a paddle-steamer berthed at Victoria Pier.

This 1836 advertisement for the King's Arms Hotel, Church Street, Douglas, is reputed to be the oldest mention of Ireland's greatest export – Guinness Stout.

The Douglas shore was used by the hoteliers to dry and air their linen. In the background is the Iron Pier, which was built in 1869 and dismantled in 1892.

In 1897 the Forrester family began to develop the resort of Port Soderick, three miles south of Douglas. Their steam-boat *Karina* is shown here passing the old Douglas Head lighthouse on its way to their resort.

Victoria Street, Douglas, before the tramlines were laid in 1896.

Henry Bloom Noble was one of Douglas's main benefactors, and paid for the construction of Noble's Hospital in 1886. When a new hospital was built, this building was transferred to the Manx Museum in 1922 and now forms the core of Manx National Heritage.

Douglas Head. The steam-ferry used to bring thousands of people across Douglas Harbour to the many amusements on Douglas Head, but not on Sundays; this was reserved for the open-air service. The tower of the hotel was a fishing mark, the hotel being built around it.

The Nunnery of St Bridget at Braddan dates from the twelfth century. The Taubman family bought it in 1797 and it stayed in the Taubman Goldie-Taubman families for many years. A recent occupant was Robert Sangster, the famous racehorse owner.

World-renowned architect Mackay Hugh Baillie Scott spent his formative architectural years designing buildings on the island. This is Oakleigh, Glencrutchery Road, Douglas.

The impressive entrance to Falcon Cliff, with its lift to the palatial hotel and dance hall. The lift was later transferred to Port Soderick.

The Isle of Man Bank headquarters on Prospect Hill, Douglas, took the place of an ugly, bill-bedecked building in 1902. Built of Aberdeen granite, the building retains its late Victorian grandeur to this day.

The launch of SS *Lady Fry* from the boatyard at the Tongue, Douglas Harbour, 22 October 1929. This was the first boat to be built at a Douglas shipyard for fifty years.

The busy harbour of Douglas Bay from the Head. The four Steam Packet paddle-steamers represent only a small section of the fleet at this time. The fishing fleet prepares for another night's fishing.

North Quay, Douglas. During the winter months, the Isle of Man Steam Packet Company paddle-steamers were berthed at the Tongue, at the head of Douglas Harbour, along with much of the local fishing fleet.

The Tower of Refuge was built by Sir William Hillary to aid sailors shipwrecked on Conister Rock. In this case it was the Isle of Man Steam Packet's SS *Mona*, which ran aground on 8 July 1930.

Mr William J. Corkill, the blacksmith, working in his smithy in Hope Street, Douglas. This building is still recognizable today. Mr Corkill was the Mayor of Douglas from 1930 to 1932.

A group of artists at a life study class, Douglas School of Art. The model is Jack Straw, a noted Douglas character, no doubt earning a few coppers for his morning's sedentary work.

A crowded Douglas harbour scene, *c.* 1906. Douglas Head ferries and Steam Packet boats jostle for water space. Whether or not Beecham's Pills were a cure for sea-sickness is not recorded!

A tipper truck! The combination of the gradient of Bank Hill, Douglas, and an overhanging load proved too much for this Electric Board truck.

Braddan New Church. Built in 1876, it had only three vicars between 1887 and 1950.

Braddan New Church. Originally designed with a large spire, it was actually built with a smaller, wooden structure. This blew off in a gale in 1884, and was never replaced. Faulty workmanship was blamed at the time.

The increased volume of traffic across the River Dhoo meant the Highway Board had to widen the Stone Bridge at the head of Douglas Harbour, seen here in November 1936, during the reconstruction.

Douglas Town Hall. The Douglas Corporation celebrated its Centenary in 1996, but they were celebrating Queen Elizabeth II's Coronation when they decorated the Town Hall in 1953.

THE WAR YEARS

The morning inspection and roll call at Douglas Camp.

The Cunningham Young Men's Holiday Camp was speedily converted into the Douglas internee camp; the huts and tents were home to the first three thousand prisoners to be sent to the island in 1914.

Prisoners waiting for food. Men collected provisions for each hut from the central kitchens. Originally built for 5,000 prisoners, Knockaloe Camp near Peel housed nearly 24,500 on Armistice Day, 1918.

Feeding the vast numbers of prisoners was a huge task; this is the meat store at Knockaloe Camp.

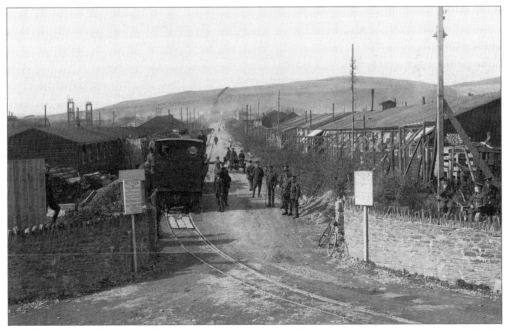

A rail link was laid into Knockaloe Camp to send in provisions and supplies. It connected with the St John's–Peel line at Glenfaba.

Knockaloe Camp post office. All mail into and out of prisoner of war camps was read, and censored if necessary.

Craftsmen internees in the Knockaloe Camp were given contracts for work. One such contract was the creation of this bedroom suite to a Charles Rennie Mackintosh design.

Winters were bleak in Knockaloe Camp.

During the First World War, the Derby Castle dance hall at Douglas was converted into a factory manufacturing, amongst other things, sections of airships and garments.

In the Second World War, the British Government decided to incarcerate enemy aliens and the Isle of Man was again chosen to house many of them This is Mooragh Camp, Mooragh Promenade, Ramsey. Opened on 27 May 1940, it housed Germans, Finns and Italians.

The Home Guard on parade on Douglas Promenade. Their main role was to patrol the many Internment Camps dotted around the island.

TRANSPORT

The Villiers Hotel coach at rest outside the Lancashire Hotel, Santon, proprietor R. Craine. Note the horn-blower on the dicky.

The Jubilee Clock and Villiers Hotel, Douglas, 1902. The cable-car in the foreground is bound for Upper Douglas while the horse-tram is taking visitors along the length of the promenade. A stiff cart threads its way between the public service vehicles.

The engine *Caledonia* at St John's station. The St John's to Foxdale line was the last track to be laid on Man, in 1883. Primarily to bring the ore out of the Foxdale mines, it also operated a school service, taking the children to St John's or connecting with the Douglas–Peel trains.

The electric tram first ran from Douglas to Groudle in 1892. The line was extended to Laxey the next year. Here, tram no. 2 takes part in a trial run to Laxey in 1893.

Douglas had a cable tramway linking the Promenade with Upper Douglas. Here, the cable tracks are being laid on Prospect Hill in 1896.

The Snaefell mountain railway, running from Laxey to the highest point on the island, was constructed in barely eight months in 1895. Here, car no. 4 stands outside the summit station and booking office in 1900. From Snaefell's summit it is said that you can view seven kingdoms: England, Ireland, Scotland, Wales and Man, plus the Kingdoms of Heaven and Neptune!

The opening of Marine Drive railway, 16 July 1896. The tramway was built to take tourists on a scenic coastal route from Douglas Head to Port Soderick.

Percy Brook at the Cronk Smithy, Ballaugh, with the first motorcycle on the island – but many thousands more have been seen here since Percy ventured forth on his pioneer steed.

Groudle Glen railway was yet another Victorian transport attraction that has survived to this day. The narrow gauge engine is shown here in about 1907 at Bear Pit Halt. The Glen's principal attractions were a sealion pool and bear pit. The railway has now been restored by private enthusiasts and trains run at weekends.

The first powered flight on the island was performed by Graham Claude White; he took to the air on 4 July 1911, and was giving pleasure flights the next day. His plane was transported in crates to the island by steamer.

The Peel–Douglas railway at Glenfaba Mill, *c.* 1911.

The end of the First World War saw a huge surplus of planes and pilots, many of whom sought to make a living from their national service. Pleasure flights around the island took off from Douglas Beach; here two Avro biplanes are waiting for customers on Queen's Promenade, August 1919. (*Photograph: A. Ainsworth*)

The only Manx-built motorcycle was the Aurora, built by J. Graham Oates in Ramsey in 1919. Oates later went on to find fame by making the first trans-Canada ride; he took to the railway lines where there were no roads. (*Photograph: Author's collection*)

G.W. Kewin, the Ramsey town surveyor, climbing into an Avro on Ramsey Beach en route for an eagle's eye view of the town, 1920.

The Isle of Man Road Services always kept up to date with their vehicles. This is a 1930 Thornycroft omnibus.

This inclined railway took the Victorian pleasure-seekers from Douglas Harbour up to the many attractions on Douglas Head. The 4 ft gauge railway was privately built and financed.

In the Second World War, the island was used for RAF training. This is a short-nose Bristol Blenheim Mk 1, belonging to No. 5 Bombing & Gunnery School, at Jurby in 1943.

When the Steam Packet boats used the Queen's Pier at Ramsey on a regular basis, a narrow gauge railway was used to take the passengers the half mile from Ramsey Promenade to the berthing head of the pier.

One horse power: a single-decker horse-tram travels along Douglas Promenade.

PEOPLE

The 'Sulby Giant', Arthur Caley, was the eleventh of twelve children. At the age of twenty-two, he stood 7 ft 6 in tall, and weighed 44 stones. He later went to Paris and finally to America, where he appeared with Barnum and Bailey's circus.

The Victorian music hall star Florrie Ford spent a great deal of time in the island; this is her bungalow at Niarbyl, on the island's west coast. It was Florrie Ford who changed the song 'Kelly from the Emerald Isle' to 'Kelly from the Isle of Man'.

Port Erin fishermen, c. 1890. The group includes men from many old Manx families, including the Cregeens, Christians and Wattersons. Generations of Manxmen have made a tenuous living on the waters around the island, fishing mainly for herring.

The island's national poet, T.E. Brown, is celebrated in this stained glass window at the Manx Museum, designed by William Hoggatt. Some of the characters from his famous poems are depicted in the three panels.

Due to the size of the Manx fishing fleet, very large amounts of ropes of various thickness were required. Here, Charlie Corkill lays the twine at a Ramsey rope walk, prior to warping it into rope lengths.

Archibald Knox, as depicted in a museum leaflet. Knox was educated at Douglas Grammar School before attending the Douglas School of Art. He left his native land to become one of the foremost designers of the English Art Nouveau movement, before returning to the island to work as an art teacher. He died in 1933.

Knox silverware. Archibald Knox, born in 1864, was a largely self-taught artist, but his watercolours were world famous. In addition to painting, he worked in silver; his use of Celtic interlacing designs is well illustrated in this superb tea service for London's House of Liberty.

Thomas Arthur Corlett Snr, with an unidentified passenger, take their ease on this early tandem on Ramsey Promenade around the turn of the century. (*Photograph: Corlett collection*)

Thomas Arthur Corlett Jnr, started his lifetime's passion for vehicles in this home-made sidecar attached to his father's acetylene-lit treader. Tommy still rode a little motorcycle well into his eighties. (*Photograph: Corlett collection*)

Sulby Glen. The large numbers of sheep roaming the Manx hills meant plenty of work for spinners. This venerable lady uses natural light; the small windows in the cottage would have precluded her working indoors.

Sir Hall Caine, the island's premier author, at his palatial home, Greeba Castle. A number of his works were turned into films, the most successful being *The Manxman*, which was director Alfred Hitchcock's last silent movie. In addition to his literary work, Hall Caine also represented Ramsey in the House of Keys.

In Hall Caine's book *The Manxman*, one of the characters was called Old Pete. John Kinnish took on the persona of this fictitious character, and used to invite passers-by into his old cottage and sell them 'souvenirs'. It was said that he had a generous supply of these 'souvenirs' stacked in the roof!

Mrs Marion Shimmin being sworn in as a member of the House of Keys, the island's Parliament, on 14 February 1933. She was the first woman member of the House of Keys, although women have had the vote in the island since 1881.

The artist William Hoggatt with his painting *Port Erin from the Artist's Garden* (1937). It was presented to the Manx Museum to mark Coronation year, 1953, and now hangs in the Museum Art Gallery.

Queen Elizabeth II and Prince Philip waving to the crowds from the balcony of Douglas Town Hall in 1955, during one of their many visits to the island in their roles as Lords of Mann.

SECTION FIVE

EVENTS

*Queen Victoria and Prince Albert paid a surprise visit to the island on the royal yacht on 20 September
1847. The Queen stayed aboard, but the Prince Regent walked through Ballure Glen to the top of Lhergy
Frissel to get a view of the island. The Albert Tower was built to commemorate the event on land donated by
Edward Stowell of Ballastowell.*

Opened in 1876 by Thomas Lightfoot, the promenade horse-tram operation was taken over by Douglas Corporation in 1907. This photograph shows the official handing-over ceremony on Thursday 2 January 1907.

Founded in 1853, Dumbell's Bank crashed on 3 February 1900, wrecking the island's economy; over 8,000 depositors were affected. Property values fell by 50 per cent. The crash left a trail of death, poverty and bankruptcy in its wake.

A meeting of the Manx Automobile Club at Kirby, Braddan, home of George Drinkwater; he was the owner of vehicle registration MN1, the first island registration number, issued on 1 January 1906.

A newly married couple set off on their honeymoon. (*Photograph: Corlett collection*)

Crowded carriages take a group of schoolchildren and teachers on a Wesleyan Sunday School picnic to Ballasalla, 1910.

A Sei whale came ashore on Langness on 8 May 1925, but it could not turn around and died where it beached. The carcase was towed behind three traction engines to Douglas – it was said that householders along the route were advised to close their windows to keep out the smell. The skeleton now hangs in the Natural History Gallery of the Manx Museum.

When Sir Hall Caine's book *The Manxman* was turned into a film, it was shot on the island, using local people as extras. Here, the extras are filming outside St John's Church in 1928.

In 1929 Castle Rushen was transferred to the Manx nation from the British Crown. Here, the castle key is being handed over.

A traditional Christmas entertainment was the White Boys' dance, performed here in the Manx Museum on 14 January 1939. It mirrors the Hobby, a dance from southern England.

A flashflood in September 1930 caused havoc in Glen Auldyn. Houses and waterwheels were swept away; this car was carried half a mile down the River Auldyn. (*Photograph: Corlett collection*)

Tynwald ceremony. The tiered mound is said to be made from soil taken from all seventeen parishes. New laws are proclaimed in both Manx and English at the open-air ceremony held on 5 July each year. The Isle of Man's ancient Parliament has close parallels in several Scandinavian countries, especially Iceland, and celebrated its millennium in 1979.

King George VI and Queen Elizabeth attending a Tynwald ceremony, as Lords of Mann. Here, the thirteenth-century Manx Sword of State is carried before the royal couple in procession to Tynwald Hill from the church.

The Queen's representative: the installation of Sir Ronald Garvey as Lieutenant Governor of the island, at Castle Rushen on 14 September, 1959.

The island has always hosted foreign dance and music groups. Here, a troupe of Norwegians is about to board a train at Douglas station en route to Peel for another dancing session.

INDUSTRIES

A road-roller on the promenade, Ramsey.

Cronkbourne Village, *c.* 1860. These workers' houses were built to house the sailmakers who worked for Moore's at the nearby Tromode Mills. This company is reputed to have made the sails for the SS *Great Britain*.

The Laxey flour mill, established by Captain Rowe, then captain of the Laxey lead mines, was opened in 1861. It caught fire many times during its working life; this picture shows the worst conflagration in 1921. However, it survived and is still processing grain to this day.

The delivery cart of Cowin's, bakers and confectioners, Onchan. It was very much a family business – John Henry Cowin stands by the horse; the two bakers are his brothers, John Caesar and James Edward.

James Creer working on his weaving loom in Colby, 1876.

The windmill at Baldromma Beg, Maughold.

Loading salt for export to Glasgow. In the process of prospecting (unsuccessfully) for coal at the Point of Ayre in 1892 a vast brine lake was discovered. This was used for fish-processing, but proved uneconomical after a few years.

In 1900 Douglas Corporation commenced the construction of the Injebreck Reservoir. Here, a train is bringing in stone cladding for the face of the embankment. The reservoir was completed in September 1905.

The engine, *West Baldwin*, at Douglas, ready to be hauled to work on the construction of the Injebreck Reservoir by a steam traction engine owned by Archie Crellin.

A Highway Board traction engine provides the saw-bench power for cutting timber at Claughbane, Ramsey, *c.* 1907.

Tom Callow, the brewer, with his dray outside the Castletown Brewery in 1910.

Three generations of the Palmer family edited and printed the *Peel City Guardian* from the basement of their newsagent's shop in Michael Street, Peel. The base of the printing press, too big to remove, still lies in the basement of the building. (*Photograph: E. Palmer*)

A steamer discharges salt at the Peel breakwater. The Scottish fish girls, seen here rolling barrels along the quay, travelled round the British Isles following the herring fleet.

Prior to 1922 there was no tarmacadam on the island roads; the surface was purely rolled and graded, hence the need for constant repair work by the Highway Board men and their steam roller.

John Clague's foundry, behind his ironmonger's premises in Parliament Street, Ramsey. Employing eighteen workers, it manufactured household goods as well as a range of cast-iron novelty items, including a model of the right hand of Arthur Caley, the 'Manx Giant' (*see* p. 35).

The generator-house of the North Quay, Douglas power station, in 1924. This power house was superseded by the Pulrose power station in 1926.

The brush department of Clucas's Laundry, Tromode, in 1930. The company is still based in the old Moore's sail makers' premises.

The packing room at Clucas's Laundry, Tromode, 1930.

Mr Kaye, farrier, shoeing Collister's carthorse at his smithy, the Cooil, Braddan, April 1937.

AGRICULTURE AND MINING

Turf cutting in Ballaugh Curragh, c. 1890. With no coal deposits in the island, peat was used by many crofters for heating and cooking. Turf is still cut today, the required licence costing £3 a year.

When their harvest was safely gathered in, the Manx farming community held a 'Melliah' or barn dance, to celebrate the end of the farming year. This photograph shows a Melliah in 1895.

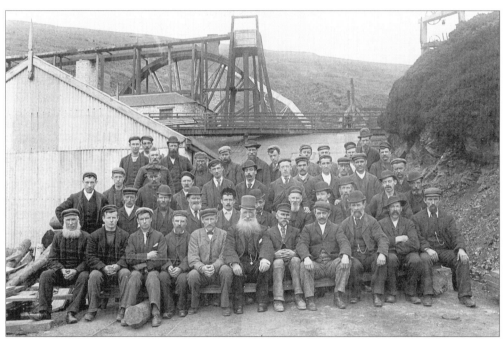

In 1897 poisonous fumes overcame a group of miners in the Snaefell mine. Twenty men died in the disaster, but the rescue team, shown here, saved fourteen men.

'Big Porker.' Johnny Joe Looney of Maughold and his blind brother were famous for breeding outsize fatstock.

Ellerslie model farm, constructed during the First World War. Italian prisoners from Knockaloe Camp were enlisted to build this very advanced farm complex.

An early Ruston combine harvester at work. It was common for a group of farmers to hire the machine and a traction engine to drive it; they would then harvest each farm in turn.

Sheep-shearing, using an early form of mechanical shears.

The island had plenty of watermills dotted along the banks of the many rivers. This is Glenfaba Corn Mill, photographed in about 1930. The Douglas–Peel railway ran alongside; the tailrace from the wheel exits left under the railway into the River Neb.

Transporting sheep to the Calf of Man, April 1952. Mr Fred Faragher had just become warden for the Manx National Trust. The sheep had an easy ride, but cattle had to swim across in the ten minutes' 'slack water' between tides.

Jimmy Cowley mending a stone wall at Cregneash Village, March 1949. The village is one of the Manx National Heritage folklife sites.

Farmer Corteen, of Thalloo Queen Farm, has no desire for motorization, as shown by this picture of his fine horse team pulling his forty-year-old reaper binder in August 1953.

The grain-milling machinery in the Garwick Corn Mill, Baldrine.

The Manx Cat is an indigenous breed, and there are many folk tales as to how it lost its tail. There are two types, the 'stumpy', which has a vestige of a tail, and the pure 'rumpy' as shown here. It is said the cats were first brought here by the Vikings.

The Loaghtan sheep, with its curious horns, is a breed unique to the island.

Snaefell mines in operation, *c.* 1890. The signboard reads: 'The Great Snaefell Mining Company, Henry James, Manager'. This mine operated from 1856 until the early twentieth century, extracting lead, silver and zinc.

Miners gathered on the washing floors at Foxdale mines, 1899.

A group of Laxey miners at the turn of the century. The miners' hats were made of felt; the candles were held fast by a cake of clay. Many of these men walked miles to the mine, worked their shift, then walked home again. Note the candles slung round their necks.

This photograph shows the 'Lady Isabella', the world-famous Laxey Wheel, in motion. Built in 1854, the wheel pumped water away from the 2,000 ft deep mine workings. The mine closed in 1929, but the wheel can still be seen turning, a monument to Victorian engineering and enterprise.

A great deal of damage was caused by a flashflood which swept through the Laxey Valley in 1930. The T-rocker viaduct of the Laxey Wheel was damaged when the arches supporting it were swept away.

The washing floors at Laxey. Water power was used to crush, wash and sort the ore. It is said that water coming down the Laxey Valley turned over twenty wheels before emptying into the Irish Sea.

The Jubilee Clock Tower, Foxdale. It looks as if it should be attached to a church, but it never was. The workings of the Foxdale mines can be seen in the background.

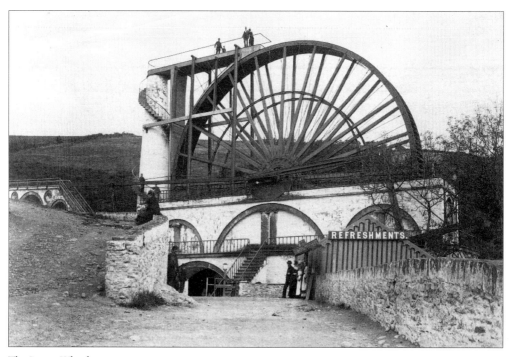

The Laxey Wheel.

SHIPS AND THE SEA

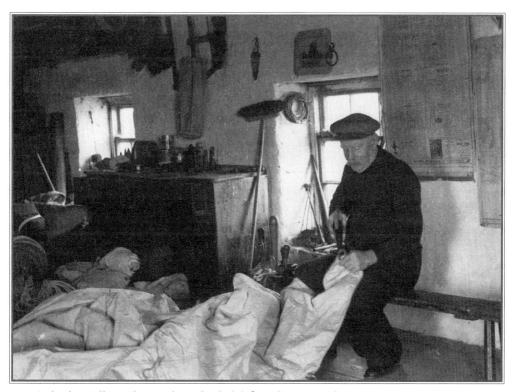

Sailmaker William Clucas in his sailmaker's loft on the Promenade, Port St Mary, October 1949.

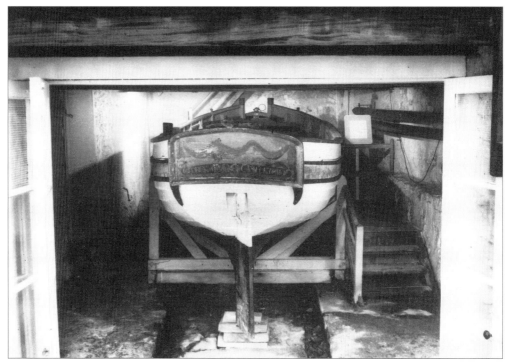

The eighteenth-century schooner-rigged yacht *Peggy*, built and operated by Captain George Quayle, was found walled-up in its Castletown boathouse in 1935. The boat and boathouse are part of the nautical history collections of Manx National Heritage.

The launch of the *Euterpe* from Ramsey shipyard, 1863. Subsequently renamed the *Star of India*, she is now the central attraction at San Diego's marine complex, and is still seaworthy.

Prior to the formation of the Coastguard, the rocket brigades were responsible for life-saving after shipwrecks. The Douglas Brigade is shown on manoeuvres at Marine Drive, *c.* 1870.

Construction of the Port Erin breakwater. The funds for the breakwater were donated by William Milner, a Liverpool safe-maker. The breakwater was destroyed in a storm in 1881. It was never rebuilt, and the jumble of tumbledown blocks still lies there.

SS *Prince of Wales* leaving the Victoria Pier. Built in 1887, she was sold by the Steam Packet Company to the Admiralty for use as a net layer in 1915.

Qualtrough's shipyard, above the Stone Bridge, Douglas.

The wreck of the Isle of Man Steam Packet vessel *Ellan Vannin* was the worst loss in the company's history. She foundered at the entrance of the River Mersey on 3 December 1909, with the loss of all crew and passengers. The wreck is immortalized in a Spinners' folksong, 'The Ellan Vannin Tragedy'.

Victoria Pier. With 29,856 visitors landing on the island in a single bank holiday in 1913, there was plenty of trade for the carriages waiting on the Victoria Pier for the next boat to arrive; the Steam Packet fleet operated a non-stop shuttle in those days.

The Wanderer. This fishing nickey, based in Peel, was within a quarter of a mile of the Cunard liner *Lusitania* when it was torpedoed by a German U-boat on 7 May 1915. Skipper William Ball and his six-man crew rescued 160 passengers and crew from the stricken liner.

The Sound separates the Calf of Man from the island. This photograph was taken during a force nine south-westerly gale. The tides are very treacherous through this narrow channel, and many vessels have come to grief on the jagged rocks.

The currents in the Sound claimed the steamship *Clan McMaster* on 30 September 1923. She ran aground in thick fog. All eighty members of the crew were saved, along with much of the cargo of cars and machinery, but the ship was lost to the elements.

Langness lighthouse. The island's many lighthouses used to be operated by the Northern Lighthouse Board, but all of them are now automatic and unmanned. The Langness light was also equipped with a fog horn.

Rose, the Douglas Head ferry, takes another bevy of visitors across the outer harbour to Douglas Head. In the background can be seen the Warwick Revolving Tower and the Camera Obscura which is still there today.

The entire complement of Manx lifeboats in Douglas Harbour, 10 May 1932, celebrating the centenary of the building of the Tower of Refuge.

The Vale O' Moray was a steam drifter, built in the days when steam power enabled the Manx fleet to sail further from the island.

In 1824 the Royal National Lifeboat Institution was founded by Sir William Hillary, a resident of Douglas. Here, the lifeboat *Civil Service No. 6* awaits the call to sea on its slipway at the Battery Pier.

A tasty morsel! This huge kipper, a gargantuan feast, measured 17½ inches long and weighed 2½ lbs when it was landed at Peel.

An 'old salt' engaged in the construction of a lobster pot. The pots were made from 'sallies' (young willow twigs), and the harvest from them gave extra, much-needed revenue to many fishing families.

Model yacht enthusiasts were older in those days. John Gawne launches his scale model of the fishing vessel *Swift* on Port St Mary boating pool in November 1938.

The *Ulster Queen*, which ran ashore at the foot of Maughold Head, 28 February 1940. It was later successfully refloated.

The Harbour Board dredger *Mannin* used to be a common sight. She worked mainly around Douglas and Peel, keeping the island's harbours free from silt and debris.

The cargo vessel *Empire Gaelic*, bringing a consignment of double-decker buses to the island for Douglas Corporation.

SUMMER PASTIMES

The Swiss Chalet, Glen Helen. The Glen was developed in 1850 by Mr Marsden, and named after his daughter. He planted thousands of trees on the banks of the River Neb, which empties into the sea at Peel.

Visitors used to ascend the Snaefell mountain by railway from Laxey. At the Snaefell Hotel, they would transfer to charabanc to go to Sulby Glen. Pictured is the earliest Snaefell Hotel.

A Manx souvenir – a popular Victorian keepsake was a three-legged sailor teapot. Most of these pots actually emanated from the Staffordshire potteries.

Sulby Glen tea gardens. The horse-drawn transport boom opened up the island's glens to the tourist. Guests would arrive at Sulby Glen from Laxey by tram and coach, then leave to return to Douglas by steam train.

Victorian swimmers were a hardy lot! The Port Skillion swimming pool, catering solely for the male population, was filled by the sea at each tide. The original Douglas Head lighthouse stands guard in the background.

Victorian amusement palaces: the Palace dance hall (foreground), with the vaulted roof of Olympia behind, and Falcon Cliff Hotel to the rear right. Olympia closed in 1896; its location, off the Promenade, was a contributory factor to its declining clientele.

There were many photographic booths in Douglas. This family portrait, with its painted backcloth of the Tower of Refuge and Douglas Head, was taken by Fred Johnson at his Fort William Studios, Douglas Head Road.

Mr T. Cowley constructed the swimming pool on the Mooragh Promenade, Ramsey. It was a popular venue for tourists and locals alike, and galas were held there.

Visitors staying at Cunningham's Camp would lodge their valises in this van, then make their way on foot to Cunningham's Holiday Camp at Victoria Road, Douglas.

Port Soderick was developed by the Forrester family, who owned the area, as a tourist attraction in the late 1890s (*see* p. 9).

In 1897 the Falcon Cliff Hotel funicular railway was bought and installed to bring customers from the newly opened Marine Drive railway down to the many amusement halls.

The Big Dipper at White City, Onchan Head, *c.* 1922. The site included Pierrot shows, along with the usual fairground sideshows and other attractions.

The Isle of Man was advertised as a holiday destination on billboards in many railway stations across Britain; this 1923 poster shows a summer scene of Peel beach, with Peel Castle in the background.

An Isle of Man Tourist Board display, with a superb scale model of the Steam Packet turbine steamer *Ben my Chree III* ('Woman of my heart').

Ballavagher House youth hostel, Union Mills. The island used to have four or five youth hostels to cater for the more energetic holiday-maker but currently there are none.

Douglas Carnival was a popular attraction for locals and tourists alike. This float was entered by the Douglas Holiday Camp.

A 1950s summer scene on Central Promenade, Douglas.

What's the Isle of Man built on? Gore's Rock, according to the legend behind the salesgirl in one of Gore's many 'rock shops' in Strand Street, Douglas. (*Photograph: A. Ainsworth*)

Park Road School dance group perform the folkdance 'Car ny Ferishyn' ('fairy dance').

RAMSEY AND THE NORTH

Bride Church and village, 1909.

Parliament Street, Ramsey, *c.* 1905. The view is still recognizable, but modern-day traffic would certainly prevent the young lad playing with his hoop in the road.

Old Laxey village and harbour. The harbour was used to transport the lead ore from the Laxey and Snaefell mines.

The old parish church of Ballaugh; note its staggered gateposts.

Ramsey was served by both electric and steam trains; the electric line ran from Derby Castle, Douglas. This print shows the electric tram terminus, still in use today, nearly a hundred years after its inauguration.

Bishopscourt, near Kirk Michael. For many centuries this house, which had its own chapel, was the home of the island's bishops. The main part of the house dates from the fourteenth century, with many additions having been made over the years.

Mooragh Park. The Mooragh Lake was formed when the course of the Sulby River through Ramsey was altered. The lake was, and still is, a popular boating pool.

The Bride post office was operated by Esther Christian from 1897 until 1920, when she was succeeded by Esther Kinrade, her daughter, who ran it until May 1963. The wall was built outside the office to deter the local lads from sitting there and distracting the girls at work.

Sulby railway station, once a popular stopping place, is now a bungalow, while the old line forms part of the network of footpaths that criss-cross the island.

The Isle of Man railway completed the northern loop from St John's to Ramsey in 1877. Here, the viaduct at Glen Mooar dwarfs a locomotive and its carriages in about 1910.

The Ramsey fish market, Market Square, Ramsey, *c.* 1910.

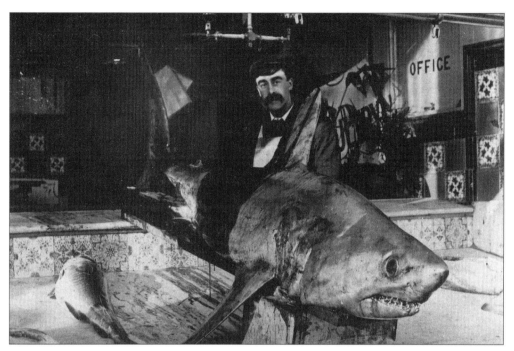

Big fish and chips! This shark must have given the fishermen a fright when they hauled it in in their nets. It was displayed at a fish shop in Ramsey.

Members of the Ramsey fire brigade and Marines form a guard of honour for a civic occasion, *c.* 1910.

Laxey Glen Gardens. The Glen Gardens were developed as an arboretum and pleasure gardens by Robert Williamson. Many majestic trees from his collection are still standing.

The Rhenass Falls, Glen Helen. The upper bridge and associated walkways have long since disappeared.

Ballaglass Glen, near Ramsey.

An evening view of Ramsey Harbour, with warehouses and fishing vessels. The Albert Tower on Lhergy Frissel can be seen at top left (*see* p. 43).

Milntown House, Lezayre. This house was formerly the country home of the Manx patriot William Christian, 'Illiam Dhone'. In later years it has served as a hotel, school and military camp, but is now in private hands.

Dhoon Glen has a most splendid waterfall and walks leading from the tramway down to the shore. The Dhoon Hotel was built of wood, as many Victorian inns were, and burnt down in April 1932.

CASTLETOWN
AND THE SOUTH

Castle Rushen and the harbour, c. 1900. Castletown was the island's capital until that honour was transferred to Douglas. A castle has stood at the mouth of the Silverburn river since the twelfth century.

The Great Clock of Castle Rushen was given to the island by Queen Elizabeth I in 1597. The clock face has only a single hand; it has caused much puzzlement to visitors throughout the ages, but still keeps perfect time.

The Smelt Monument in Castletown Square, with Castle Rushen in the background. It was originally intended to complete the monument by installing a figure of Colonel Smelt atop the column, but sufficient funds were not available. Colonel Smelt was a former Governor of the island.

King William's College. When King William was asked for a contribution to build the island's college, the only thing he gave was his name! The current college, built in 1833, has educated a great number of the island's worthy citizens.

Greeba Castle, the home of author and politician Sir Hall Caine, towers over the trees by the Douglas–Peel road. This is part of the TT course where bikes achieve speeds of over 180 mph.

The medieval Monks' Bridge, Ballasalla. Built in the twelfth century, this is the oldest bridge on the Isle of Man, and spans the Silverburn river, near Rushen Abbey.

A boat porch adorns the Cregneash village home of Neddy Beg Hom Ruy, the Manx poet, and one of the last fluent native speakers in the Manx language.

The fishing tower at Langness was long thought to be a lookout post built to guard against invasion. In fact, it was actually used as a fishing mark, as the low-lying land around Langness left the fishermen without any points of reference. The tower was duplicated on Douglas Head, but the second tower was later incorporated in the Douglas Head Hotel.

The Sugarloaf Rock, Spanish Head, has long been home to guillemots and kittiwakes, the birds that inhabit the island's craggy coasts.

One of the earliest pictures of Cregneash village, a fishing and crofting community in the south of the island, and one of the last strongholds of the Manx Gaelic language. The village is now preserved as a living folk museum.

Harry Kelly's Cottage, Cregneash village.

There has been a farmstead on the Calf of Man for over two hundred years. The premises are occupied by the Calf Warden and serve as a hostel during the summer months.

The almshouses and church at St Marks.

St Trinian's Church, Marown. Local tradition has it that the church roof was never added. Every time they tried to roof it, a 'buggane' (evil spirit) removed it.

Port Erin Bay and Bradda Head. The construction atop the head is Milner's Tower, built to commemorate the assistance given to the area by William Milner, a Liverpool safe-maker. At the foot of the cliffs is Bradda mine, which produced a great deal of lead ore.

PEEL

Peel Castle. St Patrick's Isle is dominated by the limestone fortification of Peel Castle. The Isle was separate from the 'mainland' until a breakwater was built to link it to the town of Peel in the eighteenth century, and as recently as the 1960s a ferry boat carried visitors across Peel Creek to the castle.

This is probably a posed picture, showing a spinner and net-menders. The 'pigs' appearing over the wall are 'mollags', inflated dog skins, which were used as floats for fishing nets. Peel Castle is in the background.

Peel Harbour and Castle. Although St Patrick's Isle was a separate island until the breakwater was built, folklore suggests that a tunnel used to link the two; it has never been found. The proprietor of the Fenella Hotel on Peel Hill used to fire a cannon every time a passenger boat arrived in Peel. The hotel, built in the late 1850s, burnt down on 7 November 1896, luckily without loss of life.

King Edward VII and Queen Alexandra visited Peel Castle in 1902. This photograph, taken by G.B. Cowen of Ramsey, purports to show the royal couple at the castle, but it's a fake – the figures were cut from a photograph taken at Bishopscourt, and overlaid over a painting of St German's Cathedral, an early example of photomontage.

It was said that you could cross Peel Harbour on the decks of the fishing boats. This view of the fishing fleet gives an impression of the numbers of boats that used to set sail.

Atholl Place, Peel.

A group of old fishermen on Peel Quay – what tales these men could tell about life at sea! This part of the quay is variously called 'The Parliament' or 'Weatherglass Corner' by those who congregate there, or 'Spit Corner' by others.

"The Last Muster,"

R.N.R. BATTERY,

PEEL, ISLE OF MAN.

—:o:—

**Opened March, 1884.
Closed March 31st, 1906.**

—:o:—

Greatest number belonging to Force at any one time, 650. Number drilled altogether, about 5,000.

Officers Past and Present.

Battery Officer—MR. QUIGLEY.
   ,,   MR. DAVEY.
Divisional Officer—LIEUT. NEWNHAM.
   ,,   LIEUT. LOWDAY.

Photo. D. MOUNSEY, Peel, Isle of M;

The last muster of the Royal Naval Reserve Battery, Peel Brigade, the forerunner of the Coastguard.

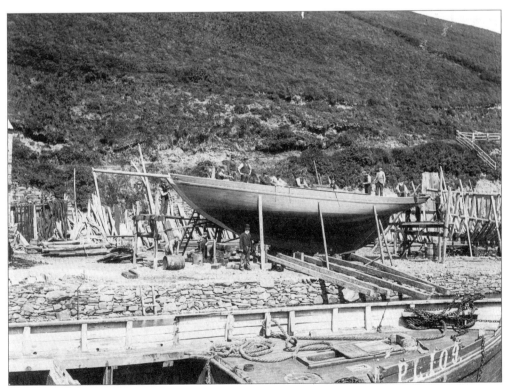

Neakle & Watterson's boatyard, under Peel Hill. The yard built many of the 'nobbies' and 'nickeys' that were the mainstay of the Manx fishing fleet.

Peel station. The first 11½ miles of track laid by the Isle of Man railway company ran from Douglas through to Peel. The service started in 1873. The station building was latterly used by the local fishermen's association, but is now intended to form part of Peel's Heritage Centre (open 1997).

Signal station, Peel Hill.

Keeping a fishing boat watertight, the crew tar the keel at low tide in Peel Creek.

Palmer's newsagents, Michael Street, Peel. (*Photograph: E. Palmer*)

The local schoolchildren at Peel used to be up at the crack of dawn on summer weekends, hurrying to get the best 'pitch' to construct their sandcastles; their hope was to catch the tourist's eye and perhaps win the odd copper. This photograph was taken in about 1908.

The Guest House, on the Headland at Peel, was used as a field hospital for enemy aliens who were billeted in Peel during the Second World War.

SPORT

Putting outside the old Golf Links Hotel, Fort Island.

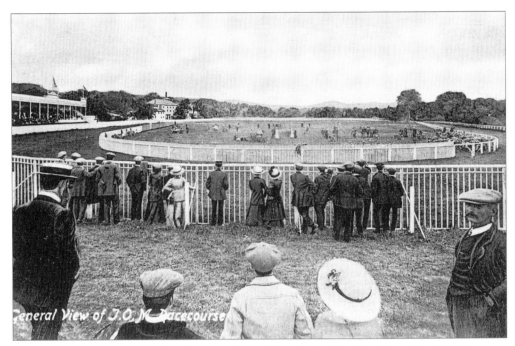

General View of I.O.M. Racecourse

The Belle Vue racecourse stood on the King George V park site, Douglas. Opened in 1912, it was a popular venue for locals and tourists alike but it was forced to close in 1931 when the Tynwald banned betting.

Athletics: this is William Quirk, running in the Andreas marathon in about 1920.

The island has hosted an International cycle race round the TT course since 1937. This is the starting line-up for the inaugural race, which was won by J. Fancourt of the Yorkshire Road Club.

The blurred machine in Peveril Road is a competitor in the TT race, which was run on a 15.8 mile circuit. Starting from St John's, the course went northwards to Kirk Michael, where it took the coast road to Peel, and thence back to St Johns.

Spaniard Victor Naure takes his Bristol-built Douglas outfit round the Ramsey hairpin in the 1925 Sidecar TT; he retired in the race.

Jimmy Guthrie pushes his Norton off at the start of the 1935 Senior TT. Guthrie was to finish second, four seconds behind Stanley Woods (Guzzi).

South African Ray Amm takes Quarter Bridge at speed on his Norton on his way to victory in the 1954 Senior TT.

Geoff Duke weighing in his Gilera for the 1954 Senior TT; he finished second. Geoff was subsequently honoured with an OBE for services to motorcycle racing.

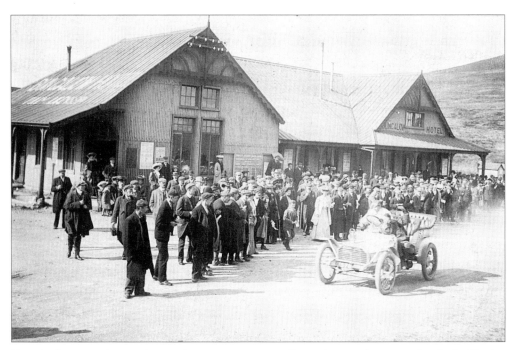

Crowd safety seems low on the agenda, as spectators surge forward to watch a competitor in the Gordon Bennett race pass the Bungalow Hotel, Snaefell.

Pitstop action at Ramsey. No. 6 is Louis Coatelen (Hillman Coatelen) and No. 18 is James Reid (Beeston Humber).

The year 1922 saw the last round-the-island car race; it would be another eleven years before racing cars made another appearance on the island. This is F.C. Clement at Ramsey hairpin; he finished second.

Motor racing was held on several true 'round-the-houses' circuits around Douglas between 1933 and 1953. In this shot, the competitors have just rounded Greensill's Corner on the promenade and are heading up Church Road.

The 1950 British Empire Race was run in appalling weather; this prang took place at Parkfield Corner on the first lap, just a few hundred yards from the start.

ACKNOWLEDGEMENTS

Since moving to the island, the author has attended many evening classes, walks and talks on its history, which have helped to foster a consuming interest in, and love of, all things Manx.

Thanks are due to many people, especially the late Sheila Cregeen, also Frank Cowin and Peter Kelly, whose love of their native land and generous sharing of their knowledge have assisted with the production of this book.

A large number of photographs have been made available by the Manx Museum, and I would like to record my thanks to their library staff, in particular Roger Sims, the Chief Librarian. I am indebted to the following for allowing me to plunder their private collections in search of further images: Audrey Ainsworth, Robin and Mrs Corlett, and Emily Palmer.